FROM THE DEPTHS OF RED BLUFF

FROM THE DEPTHS
OF RED BLUFF

To Rick,
with admiration
for a fellow poet!

A Collection of Poems

Wynne Huddleston

Mississippi Poetry Society's
2014 Poet of the Year

Mississippi Poetry Society, Inc.
Little Rock, MS

Printed in the United States of America

Cover Photos by Donna Huddleston Smith

Library of Congress Cataloging-In-Publication Data

Huddleston, Wynne.
From the depths of red bluff; by Wynne Huddleston.—1st ed.
ISBN: 978-0-9840483-2-8
Library of Congress Control Number: 2014906274

Mississippi Poetry Society, Inc.
Little Rock, MS

For my parents.

*To the wisest, most honorable man I know, my dad, DQ
Huddleston, who advised me to "plow a straight row,"
and then stood by to guide me back whenever I swayed.*

*And to the finest lady and most perfect homemaker I
know, my mom, Faye Estes Huddleston, who showed me
by example that with faith, education and hard work I
could accomplish whatever my heart desired.*

CONTENTS

Granddaughter of Make-Do / 1
Where Muscadines Grow / 2
Sweet Sunny Summers / 3
Secret of the Shell / 4
Consequence / 5
Set in Our Ways / 6
Same Stars, Different Houses / 7
I Can't Stop Loving You / 8
The Magic of Mississippi / 9
Mother's / 10
His Shirts / 12
Blue / 13
Devil's Due / 14
All We Like Sheep / 16
Endless Nights in the River Bed / 17
Closure / 18
Wedding Cactus / 19
Depressing Yourself / 20
How to Beat the Blues in 12 Bars / 21
Bittersweet / 22
My Eclipse / 23
Scattered Among the Ashes / 24
Frustrating Rewrite / 26
User and Spouse / 27
Concerto / 28
Where Eyes Are Clouds That Weep / 29
The Child / 30
Child of Mime / 31
Scraping the Surface / 32
Its Mark / 33
For Sale: Memory for a Song / 34
Chorus of Children's Voices / 35
I Am / 36

Between Us / 37

Regret / 38

Blessing / 39

Acceptance / 40

Feeding the Ghost of You / 41

Crushed / 42

October / 43

From the Depths of Red Bluff / 44

No Matter / 46

The Sands of My Life / 47

Summer of the Centipedes / 48

Fishing at Midnight / 49

Trees at Play / 50

Five Winter Haiku / 51

Barefoot in the Snow / 52

What Do You Know of Spring? / 53

Circle of Eternity / 54

Fisted River / 55

ACKNOWLEDGMENTS

My thanks to the publications in which these poems, or earlier versions of these poems, first appeared.

Southern Women's Review: "Granddaughter of Make-Do"

From the Porch Swing: "Where Muscadines Grow" and "Consequence" (as "Grandpa, King of Checkers")

Mad Swirl: "Secret of the Shell"

Mississippi Poetry Society Contest Journals: "Sweet Sunny Summers," "Devil's Due"—MPS Award, "I Can't Stop Loving You," "Mother's," "Its Mark," "The Child," "My Eclipse," "User and Spouse," "Between Us," "Regret," "What Do You Know of Spring?" and "Circle of Eternity"

Eskimo Pie: "Set in Our Ways" and "I Am"

Deep South Magazine: "Same Stars, Different Houses," Pushcart Nomination

Today in Mississippi: "The Magic of Mississippi"

Birmingham Arts Journal: "His Shirts"

Short, Fast and Deadly: "Blue"

Camroc Press Review: "Closure," "Depressing Yourself," and "October"

Indigo Rising: "Endless Nights in the River Bed"

THEMA: "How to Beat the Blues in Twelve Bars" (mistakenly credited to another author)

Heavy Hands Ink: "Concerto" and "Fisted River"

The Rainbow Rose, "Where Eyes Are Clouds That Weep," and "Crushed"

Orange Room Review: "Scraping the Surface"

Ink, Sweat & Tears: "For Sale: Memory for a Song"

WestWard Quarterly: "Chorus of Children's Voices"

Mused: Bella Online Literary Journal: "Acceptance" and "Trees at Play"

Halfway Down the Stairs: "Feeding the Ghost of You"

joyful!: "The Sands of My Life"

Eunoia Review: "Summer of the Centipedes"

Words: A Poetry and Prose Anthology: "Fishing at Midnight"

EarthSpeak: "Barefoot in the Snow"

Poppy Road Review: "Five Winter Haiku"

Thank you to my entire family who has shown me so much love and encouragement on this journey. Hugs to my wonderful grandchildren Julia and Jude who fill me with inspiration.

Thanks to my aunt, Dr. Bonnie Ivey and to Linda for leading me in the right direction. Love to Joey, my constant support!

Thanks to the Mississippi Writers Guild. Many of my poems were shaped by their workshops led by Dr. Angela Ball, Irene Latham, Sandra Beasley, and others.

To my teachers: B.F. Blass, for all the poems I had to memorize in grade school, Bernice Huddleston, in whose 6th grade class I wrote my first "real" poem, to John Turner, Dr. Robert Pawlowski, and Dr. Joe Taylor— thanks for your instruction and encouragement!

Thank you to MPS and the wonderful poets of Central Branch for nominating me for Poet of the Year, but most of all for the joyful fellowship during our meetings.

GRANDDAUGHTER OF MAKE-DO

I am the sturdy granddaughter of brush brooms,
apron strings, caramel icing, well water, fresh
cow's milk, green pastures, cornfields, pea patches,
red dirt roads, peaches (and switches) right off
the tree, hard child birthing at home, family
Bibles, Sunday meetings, hugs and kisses, treats
from the peddler's wagon, bare feet, squealing
pigs, mean chickens, pallets with cousins
on the floor, front porch swings with guitars,
fiddles and singing, swept yards, make-do
attitudes, country stores, letters to politicians,
hard work for little pay, feet soaked
in a porcelain bowl, homemade clothes,
European immigrants, fireplaces, no air
conditioning, outhouses, checkers, snuff,
and wishes blown away on a dandelion.

WHERE MUSCADINES GROW

Grandpa picks a cape jasmine and pins it
on his jacket, tips his hat, and offers me
peppermint that he buys from the peddler's
wagon. Deaf, not dumb, he gives me
secret winks, prickly pear hugs, green apples,
purple plums, and teaches me
how to play with funny things
like rolly polly bugs. Then he takes me
across the red dirt road to show me
where muscadines grow,
and how to bite through the thick, bitter skin
to find the juicy sweet pulp within.

SWEET, SUNNY SUMMERS

Sweet, sunny summers of blackberry pie,
Red Light, Green Light, and Mother May I?
Chickening out halfway through
I'll show you mine if you...
Parting the wind with the wheels
of my bike, puppy at my heels
lost in the woods right behind my own house,
climbing mimosa trees... falling out,
quiet as a mouse, no, a worm, while Pop
watches the news. Chores for Mom—
folding towels, making beds, being swung
on a quilt and then flung
on the bed, clutching sis, watching TV
afraid of the monkeys, afraid to see
the wicked witch on the *Wizard of Oz.*
On Sunday, church is scary, too, because
of all the hell-fire preaching
and the creepy cemetery, boo! Swinging
on the front porch at Grandma and Grandpa's,
listening to my uncles playing guitars
and fiddles until the fat frogs croaked,
and the beach ball sun finally broke
and bounced out of sight just behind
the spiky black gate of giant pines.

SECRET OF THE SHELL

In my dream, my mother and I are
outside Grandma's old, painted-white house;
inside, the remains of my uncle, a pilot, lie
in a casket, lid closed.
He's in heaven now, they say.
I see his airplane in the fathomless blue
and imagine it
coming straight toward us! There will be
no escape. I am just a child. I run
to the back yard, where the dirty
green sea threatens to spew out
its secret. With a thousand voices
it whispers in canon
words I cannot comprehend.
It raises a salty hand to beckon,
Come here, and teasingly holds out
a Conch shell, as though there is
something
in the hollow spiral of sound;
something
in the emptiness
it wants me
to go inside
and see.

CONSEQUENCE

There were many wooden cases
of Dr Peppers in Grandpa's country store.
When they were empty he'd turn them over
to make a table and chairs for playing checkers.
He was king at blocking the board, but
when he played with me, we didn't keep score;
he'd show me where I should make my next move,
and explain why. He taught me how to patiently
play out every possibility in my mind first,
and what would happen if I jumped too fast
without thinking about the consequence.

SET IN OUR WAYS

Gnarled and knotted
like pine, Grandma is
down to brass,
rather, plastic, knuckles.
Back bent from always
tending to others, pride
petrified like stone,

unbending
stubborn refusal
of help from dad. Meeting
of two bones joined
ball and socket,
like an eye

roll, pain
at the mere thought
of moving, losing
independence,
scream of brakes, metal
against metal slowing, bone
against bone struggle, joint cushions
gone. Why should the elderly
have to bend? We are set
in our ways in the end.

SAME STARS, DIFFERENT HOUSES

for Diane

We planned to run away, but never did. I
lived as a hermit in a new brick house full
of doors, sisters that shut me out, a nagging
mom who did everything, and a dad
who was miles away at work, or at home
booming, *Don't do this!* or *Why did you do*

that? You, my friend, subsisted in a house
of ill repair, with a present, but miserly father
who favored sons over daughter. Your mom,
imposing Cinderella chores, had been taken
by your father's uniform and promises
of seeing the world. Now a bitter,
middle-aged woman, who'd yet to cross
the ocean, was stuck in an old house with no

plumbing. But it was lovely once. It hugged us
with its wrap-around porch, it intrigued us
with its hole-in-the-roof skylight
above your bed. Whenever I'd spend the night
we'd lie there looking through it and wish
for a man who would promise
those same stars to us.

I CAN'T STOP LOVING YOU

A *Teddy Bear* with swivel hips,
sideburns that lead to curly lips,
a million come to hear him sing,
girls scream and faint to see the King.
Although he likes to have his fun,
his heart belongs to only one.

Black velvet paintings frame his face
in Delta blues, *Amazing Grace*.
A *Hound Dog* dressed in *Blue Suede Shoes*
in Mississippi, paid his dues.
Blue Christmas meant nothing new,
the same as *In the Ghetto*, too.

You're just a hunk of *Burning Love,*
so if you're listening up above,
I want *My Way*, so *Don't be Cruel.*
I'm All Shook Up and hoping you'll
Love Me Tender, Love Me True…
Elvis, *I Can't Stop Loving You.*

THE MAGIC OF MISSISSIPPI

depends on many things—
cricket songs, watermelons,
and front porch swings,

prayers whispered inside
a little country church,
our deep, muddy river,
red clay and fertile dirt,

cattle in the pasture,
catfish ponds and pines,
the smell of honeysuckles,
plums and muscadines,

the orange harvest moon,
soulful music in the air,
a white magnolia blossom,
and days with little care.

MOTHER'S

I am my mother's doll—acting at her command,
hugged not too tightly, and punished when I don't
obey. She fixes my hair like hers, dresses me
in homemade clothes. My words are spoken in her
tone of voice; her pink lipstick forms my lips. She
drags me up the narrow, wooded path, pushes me
toward God and the things she desires—I see
the world through her eyes. She points out
sharp rocks, and tells me that Morning Glories are

really invasive vines. We go to the garden where she
tells me to only pick what is ripe, and how to feel
for maturity of peas in a pod, and golden-haired
corn. She tosses me a sweet peach, right off
the tree, and picks figs for preserves. She gives me
the recipe for delicious pie made with sour green
apples and lots of sugar. Soon I am old enough to go
to college to develop my brain and God-given
talents. I snowball down the well-trampled path,

bitten by the strange and the curious. Glad to get away
from the country of work and Proverbs and sun, I
dress myself in the fad of the moment, lips painted
Siren Red. I study and learn the web of the world,
make friends with different views. They stuff me
with spicy foreign food intended to shatter
the plate from which Mother fed me. I chew on it
and decide which agrees or not with my stomach.
Then one night I throw most of it up. The next

morning I wake up and look in the mirror to put on
my usual makeup... but I stop in shock to see *her*
natural beauty stamped on *my* face; to hear *her*
tongue lash judgments from *my* mouth; to feel

10

the healing itch and pull of the stitches of wisdom
she'd sewn into the fiber of my soul. I race barefoot
down that rocky path, back to the garden to find
myself. Choosing the mature, preparing the tried
and true recipes, with some spices of my own, I know
one day I'll drag my own sweet baby doll here, too.

HIS SHIRTS

Dress shirts, size 17.
I bought this one for him,
deliciously soft,
the expensive kind
of cotton, blue and white stripe,

athletic fit. I pick it up,
breathe in his cologne,
his deodorant... his scent.
I check the pocket,

nothing there. I wear it naked,
roll up the cuffs, don't button,
wrap it around, hug myself,
dance about... I'm here.

Reluctantly, I take it off,
wash it, dry it, iron it carefully—
with steam, no starch.
I hang it facing left, button
the top two, skip to the fourth,
put it in the closet and wait for him;
to wear him once more.

BLUE

We painted the ceiling of our first home blue—
true blue,
sky blue,
baby blue...
now the paint is chipping;
pieces trash
the floor.

DEVIL'S DUE

Devil's gonna get his due;

on Highway 61, he stirred up
tornados, put us through hail, and threw
rain at Old Man River 'til he swoll up
in such a rage
from Illinois, to Louisiana
through the Mississippi Sound, now he's
goin' ag'in the law of nature—
pushin' up,
instead of flowin' down the Arkansas.

Devil's gonna get his due;

chasin' deer and ants right out o' the fields,
swallowin' our homes, drinkin' the catfish
ponds, takin' Rolling Fork, eatin' acres
and acres of cotton, sweet corn,
soybeans, and wheat planted
in the fertile Delta
soil with the sweat and toil
of the poor and the rich alike.

Devil's gonna get his due;

floodin' Muddy Waters'
playground, and Elvis', too, messed up
them blue suede shoes. Hear the music
shake and shiver—a sorrowful
tune; our Blue Delta's cryin'
a Mississippi River.

Devil's gonna get his due;

ev'rybody come to Vicksburg
to watch it, too. Gonna see if it's
bad as the flood in '26-'27. They ain't
waitin' for the levee to break, no,
they done blowed it up to save
the big cities, left us
country folks to soak it up… but we ain't
complainin' 'cause we know

Devil's *always* gonna get his due.

ALL WE LIKE SHEEP

Sheep only drink where the waters are still,
But follow wherever they're led.
Ignoring the danger up over the hill,
Sheep only drink where the waters are still.
Yet, wolves can fool them at their will,
Deceiving the herd, 'til the wool is shed.
Sheep only drink where the waters are still,
But follow wherever they're led.

ENDLESS NIGHTS IN THE RIVER BED

There is no division between
day and night in this divided
house. When sun tries to rouse
me, with its rising, I cover
my head. Clocks have no affect—
antidepressants do not care
if it's 12 a.m. or 12 p.m.; I pull
the cover over my blank face, knowing
my ghost will arise for the children's
sake—cook food, comb hair, send them
to school. She even goes to work, speaks
in monotone, drags through necessities,

the transparency of agony spooks
away the crowd. When she returns,
she rejoins me in the restless river
bed, drowns her eyes, stubs her toes
on the loose stones of despair, guilt,
and lies, groping blindly for a still
place in the gossiping

rush of water. Pray the nights and nights,
oh! endless nights will pass and it
will all be over soon! But the ever-flowing
river whispers, *Never, dead*
lover; divorce is the death scene
that goes on and on... the pain never
ends; the bodies are never laid
to rest. I stop
fighting, lie back on the water. Let it
take me where it will.

CLOSURE

Snaps, buttons, zippers, bows,
tape, staples, envelopes…
There you go, and here I sigh
wondering how to say goodbye.

WEDDING CACTUS

The cactus that Auntie gave us for our wedding
shower grew bigger and greener, flowering
into bright red blooms, faithfully
each year while we were

married. It only needed water once a month,
to thrive in so much sun and infertile
soil. But many things were left untended

after the divorce. The day you told me
you were getting married again I noticed,
tears, water, too late—

there would be no more buds.
I found it lying
on its back, dry roots up,
begging to be buried.

DEPRESSING YOURSELF

Depression lends
itself
to surrender,
I mean
you feel
ugly and
unhappy—
what's the point
in getting
dressed or putting on
makeup
or combing
your hair?
It's much
easier
to face
the enemy
when you've gone
over to
their side.

HOW TO BEAT THE BLUES IN 12 BARS

Sweeten your misery in sixteen beats,
state what you were doing, sing it three times
in disbelief—first in the tonic, then change
the point of view in the key of the subdominant,
as if to ask, *How on Earth did this happen?*
Conclude, *It just did...* and that's the truth,

so restate it in tonic as a matter of fact. What else
can we expect in this world? It ain't never gonna
change, but we can take that misery the world
dishes out just a little bit easier when we mix
it up and rearrange it into a sweet little tune.

I was pouring my coffee... early this morn',
yeah, I was [*minding my own darn business*]
pouring my coffee, early this morn', I was
pouring my coffee when you knocked me
to the floor. *Now you're singing the blues!*

BITTERSWEET

Again into your lap I pour
my seedy, bitter blackberries.
You take them and mix them
with honey and flour,
then produce the most beautiful
pie. *Lemonade?* you inquire.

Why thank you, I say,
I always have lemons, you know.
Why do you have stores of honey,
but all I possess is bitter?

*Perhaps you're too quick to pick
the green fruit in the midst of briars,
while I patiently rob honey bees.*

That's true, and I always get pricked!
But why don't you ever get stung—
because you wear mask and gloves?

Oh, no, she smiles, *they never bite,
I believe they won't...
so they don't.*

MY ECLIPSE

When reality is too painful, I simply
black it out
like a solar eclipse. I don't mean
the kind of blackout I had
when my ex slammed me, but

like when you cover
your child's wound with a Band-Aid,
so they forget it's there;

like when you get a blood test:
it doesn't hurt so much if you don't look;

like when you go to funerals and sit
behind flowers to block
the view of the front pew.

An eclipse is even better
than the antidepressants
the doctor prescribed
during my divorce!

It's like when I was at work
and someone told me
my house was on fire... I turned
my car radio up loud as it would go
so I couldn't hear myself crying
all the way back to my...

SCATTERED AMONG ASHES

I am scattered among the ashes of my
home. Nothing is the same; I search
for special things—like my old baby doll
with missing toes and hair. Oh!
there's Bugs Bunny... well, just his foot. Good
luck? No. I see his mutilated body strewn, gray
puffs of fur. No more, *What's up, Doc?* I feel
nauseated. My sons' baby pictures stare
at me, imprisoned under the smoked

glass... nothing much left
but the frame. Now I wake up each morning
disoriented, in a strange place that's not
my bedroom, not facing the rising
sun of the East. Again, I go back to dig
through the rubble, feeling like I've stumbled
through a star gate into another
dimension. The molecules of my body dis-
assemble and reassemble, each time

finding that another memory
is lost. It's hard to tell the ceiling
from the floor, but the fireplace remains.
My son and I used to sit in front of it, looking
for pictures in the stones' shapes—a cat,
an Indian, a shoe, or a boat. Up above it
was the loft with big window where I could

look out to see turkey or deer in the pasture.
On the desk was an antique oil lamp
from Great-Grandpa's barn—the kind
with bubbles in the glass—now burst
from the heat. The attic was where

I'd stupidly stored precious keepsakes—
ornaments, dolls, scrapbooks, baby clothes, but...
Praise God! My one-eyed Teddy Bear winks
at me. I go out the "door," hugging him close,
as I walk through the rubbish of broken

glass, charred wood, and trash. But there
in the midst of the black charcoal ash I see
one surreal amaryllis standing
on bare, green stem, holding up
its delicate, blood red cup
full of tiny fertile seeds.

FRUSTRATING REWRITE

Trying to find the missing piece of a jigsaw puzzle
that fell into a box of pieces of another puzzle—
wrong shape
different color—
I get frustrated. On the wall
I see a place where the sheetrock
is cracked.

Like hemming the too-long, silk pants my mother gave me.

Why don't you wear them? she asks.
The material feels wonderful.

USER AND SPOUSE

for Jim

My computer calls me user,
and I suppose I am;
early in the morning I get online,
and stay there until dawn.
It wants to find out
with whom I converse, which sites
I like to visit—it even reads
my emails. It anticipates
my needs, tells me where to go,
and sometimes locks me out—
when I can't remember my own name...
or the magic password. Smarter than I,
it corrects my errors, but if I go
where I shouldn't, it freezes up
and refuses to communicate with me...
I think I'll call it "spouse".

CONCERTO

I was flute in the orchestra sitting
stiffly in a steel chair, playing
what was written, blending in; you were
piano, soon stating your intention. I
accompanied you in an exposition
of tender passion, but after a time,
problems started to develop,
things became strained. You wandered
away; I felt lost. Then you completely

abandoned me. Going solo,
you shined in the spotlight, striking
whatever keys you chose, improvising
on what used to be our theme, then,
after a shameless display, you
had the audacity to try to recap
what we had in the beginning. Well,
it can never be the same, but I'll play
along, with my head held higher,
because I know the score...
the coda is coming soon.

WHERE EYES ARE CLOUDS THAT WEEP

My car kidnaps me, takes
me there—to the last
graveyard where the tombstones read,
Joy and *Hope,*
where my eyes are clouds that weep
upon grass that will never
again be green, and the cut
flowers there will never
fall to seed.
I tiptoe back
to the car; careful not to wake
Despair who lies
in wait in the ashy forest just beyond
the cemetery gate with your choice
of pills or
shiny revolver.

THE CHILD

The child is only five years old.
She cries, but no one seems to care.
She may be scared; she may be cold.

Her father says, *Do what you're told!*
Now, hush! I have no time to spare.
The child is only five years old.

She needs a hug, a hand to hold,
Someone to notice and declare
That she is scared; that she is cold.

When night creeps in with shadows bold,
So comes the wolf, oh, don't you care?
The child is only five years old!

Be still. Attend her needs, don't scold!
Her cries are more than I can bear—
She might be scared; she might be cold,

Ignored, neglected, uncontrolled.
At last I see through my despair;
The child in me is five years old...
And I am scared. I am cold.

CHILD OF MIME

I will speak this to you
In cliches, trite, but true.
You've nothing to invent—
It's already in print.

From May to September,
So you will remember,
How those memories burn...
Do we really live and learn?

A walk down memory lane
Will surely drive you insane.
Just eat the cake and have it, too.
Under the sun, nothing's new.

Far be it from me
To speak of eternity—
How rustling leaves fall;
Bitter winter, bitter gall;

Of eggs put in one basket,
Soft lining in a casket.
Ashes to ashes, dust
To dust, do what you must.

One day at a time, one more chink
In the wall, just one more drink.
A penny saved is a penny earned.
Still, there's nothing we have learned.

Seems there's no reason or rhyme
To Mother Earth, Father Time.
Child of Mime, child of mine,
Follow His footsteps. Rise and shine!

SCRAPING THE SURFACE

When I was small I thought
"skyscraper" referred to a jet plane,
and that the entrails were places
where the plane had actually scraped
the sky's surface, like a Magic
Writer toy. When people said, *Look,
a jet!* I couldn't find it unless
there was a big X to mark
the spot. But when I got glasses, things changed—

I could see
that a jet can never scratch or write
upon the fathomless sky.

I found out
that skyscrapers are buildings
as tall as Jack's beanstalk, but they never
will touch the sky;

I could even read the movie credits on the TV—
I discovered
that the character I thought was "Wide Earth"
was really Wyatt Earp. What a bummer...

Now, much older, I sometimes take off
my glasses and imagine what I might write
on the ceiling of the sky if I were
Wide Earth riding in a skyscraper.

ITS MARK

In my search
for beauty I stump
my toe upon an ugly stone,
I curse and pick it up to toss it off
my path, but then a voice inside screams,
Stop! I hold it close, then put it in the pocket
near my heart, because it bears the dint of some
small life that touched it once. Oh, how it must
have strived alone in its last breath to press
itself against the ageless rock, and having
left its tiny mark found rest. And so, this
lovely stone I'll keep, for when I touch
the deep impression there, I know,
if only for me, once more,
it breathes.

FOR SALE: MEMORY FOR A SONG

My grandparents' house has been sold and moved
to a remote corner in the left hemisphere
of my brain, but Chopin's *Nocturne in e minor* has never
left my fingers. My cousin lost her alphabet, the evil
joker Stroke erased the board, but the words
married to melodies remain on her lips.

Funny how I can't retrieve the data file of our second
kiss. But I vividly recall the first one, because *Wake Up,
Little Suzie* was on the radio. Yes, I'm laughing, thinking,
hypnosis might do the trick—forget it all, forget
I ever met you...

But when I am old and you are still
not here
let me ride back in time on the notes of a song—
let me think
you are.

CHORUS OF CHILDREN'S VOICES

Pitch, tenuous as a clarinet's reed—still wet,
easily broken or split—vibrates in the wind.
Tone, diction, and emotion as one; cherubic
pure, virginal soprano. Melody floats
like a kite, to untested heights, held by a fragile
string. Tempo, like one flock of many
geese, flaps trusting wings. Then dissonant
harmonies darken the sky like gentle rain,
increasing, roaring thunder *crescendos* louder,
and louder, deafening! Until, at last...
blessed sun breaks through the darkness
with a climax of intense, permeating
light. The resolution reverberates in the silent
dark places of your soul like a bright golden bell
struck and silenced at once by a single hand.

I AM

chalk rock that crumbles
    when you step on it;
fermented grapes
    that flavor your wine;
a hard diamond with one
    disfiguring split;
the furtive thorn
    on the blackberry vine;

wild violets surprising
    a silent, gray wood;
a great oak waiting
    inside an acorn;
the shoulders on which
    you wept, then stood;
the star-crossed lover
    you mourn.

BETWEEN US

While we await the birth of our first
grandchild, you refuse
to look at me. You stare at the wall
behind me as if it were

between us. I imagine
that's where you want to bury
me—in the mud and mortar between
the bricks you used to throw
when we were married. Nevertheless
I am still in your world, not
buried, but cremated, scattered

in fragments of memories—some blocked,
some remaining, like the stubborn
stains on the boxed-away wedding
gown. But this one we will keep
dear—our son enters the room, holding

this new life; we rush to stand
on opposite sides
of him. Our grandson looks at me
with your eyes, then
reaches for you
with my hand.

REGRET

Regret is the dirt swept
into a corner, the plant
you forgot to water, the engagement
ring returned to the shop, the annoying
pebble in your shoe, the unused
good china, the noisy cricket
in the middle of the night, the dirty
dish left in the sink, the book you meant
to read, the letter you should
have written, the unmade
bed, the sigh at the end of a long day,
the "I love you" you never did say.

BLESSING

I pace the floor of my new house,
from room to room I roam.
I buy new drapes, new bed, new couch—
still longing for my old home.

Like Jacob, I wrestle all night
with self, or angels or God,
but I've yet to get, by morning light,
a blessing, a stairway, or even a nod.

I do not seek redemption
in anyone's eyes but mine,
but mercy in this self-made prison
would be a blessing divine.

ACCEPTANCE

Sleep's blindfold falls
hours before dawn. In the dark I feel
for it, but yet another old sin snags
my satiny sheets like a jagged
fingernail. Gets me
out of bed, searching
in the red-peppered blackness
for a file to smooth it. I must

turn on the light to examine the offense
of my nails, my hands, then ask
God if there is
water holy enough to heal
this damage. How well I know
the skin that stretches
across these hands, thinner each year, losing

the ability to forget
to retract. Now it climbs
over years of brittle bones, it hangs
at the painful junctures, and leaves
a host of crevices from which regret can
escape. No balm can absolve

the guilt of these hands, nor restore
their innocent beauty. No polish can
stop the snag of remembered sin; but
I have found a worthy file—
acceptance. And this is all I have
to grasp, and all I have
to give.

FEEDING THE GHOST OF YOU

You return to see if I have anything left
you can devour; I protest, but you take me
in your hands, molding me into what you
desire. You pick at me with your forked
tongue, sauté me in sugar and spices, fill me
with wine, then put me in the fridge to keep
until the next bewitching hour. I sleep
only during the day, watch TV with all
the lights turned on, until I believe
you are gone for good. Then one night you
materialize from nowhere with your silver
spoon, dish out your sad story on me. Slowly
I warm to your fire—I want to fight, I want
to remember, to torture myself. After you get me
cooking, you take out the carving knife to see
if there's any heart left in me. Suddenly
I understand… you will not leave me
alone until you have picked me clean
to the bone. I crawl away, and try to excise
your evil memory. Slowly
I heal, gather heart. A shadow falls
across the wall. Here you come, again.

CRUSHED

How I wish I had drown the little bird
as soon as it had hatched... No, I should have
squashed the egg before it was born,

before I spent hours keeping it
warm against my heart;

before I watched it beat its head
through the protective shell;

before I watched its wet down fluff into feathers
on capable wings that took it up, up so high,
soaring excitedly into the blue, blue sky;

before you shot it down. Yes, I should have

crushed the shell into shards,
stomped it into the ground,
while the bird was still
just a foolish idea.

OCTOBER

the last trip to some unknown place
the last squeeze of lime in the Tequila
the last unforgettable melted-crayon sunset
the last green apple core rotting on the ground
the last crunchy leaf that finally let go
the last time you held me to your heart
the first blow of cold against my face

43

FROM THE DEPTHS OF RED BLUFF

It's like waking from a nightmare—the haunting
kind that returns in pieces, images floating
like confetti in air. I chase them, try to fit them
together: Blue—eyes, ocean. Black—phone
unanswered. Red—wine, valentine. Gold—her hair, my
promised ring. Green—picnic, jealousy. Each revelation

a blow to my sucker-punched gut. Can't eat, can't
sleep, can't stop punishing myself for letting
my heart sing, *At last*. But here you come, friend,
to rescue me, stuff my tangled curls under a skull
cap, wrap me in a jacket, strap on a helmet, and take me
on the back of your bike before sunrise, on a Sunday, past
a deserted church. I imagine people seated inside, full

of faith, singing *Amazing Grace.* I hear nothing. Confetti,
trees, pavement blur in the numbing cold. I hang on
tighter as you drive me to "Mississippi's Little Grand
Canyon," Red Bluff. Right off the road it plunges, gouged
out by the Pearl River, the vein that runs from the heart
of Mississippi, and empties into the ocean. Drip by drip,

blow by blow, erosion eats away, taking soil, sand, gravel
and clay from the broken mountain. We arrive in the gray
silence of morning for the viewing. I frown at the trash. Why
doesn't the state take care of this place? *It's privately owned,*

you tell me, *but kids party here. It's always changing;
see the trees trying to survive on the edge? They'll hang on
'til they get too weighty, then they'll fall, knocking down
a peak or two. Sometimes they destroy the road, so it has
to be rerouted, rebuilt, regardless of cost.* I lean close to
the edge, 400 feet down. I know this place. A crow cautions.

shadows shimmy and run. Then Sun breaks through
the oppressive dome to display red-crimson-pink, white,
orange-yellow-gold, green-lime, blue-indigo-violet—
all my confetti colors glowing from the depths
of Red Bluff, harmonious as God's promised bow.

You understand my silence; you've been here
before. Moisture glistens down its face,
as on mine. Now, I hear it... the music vibrates
in my bones. Here, in *this* church. *Just as I
Am*. Marvelous. Beautiful. Amazing. Grace.

NO MATTER

Stars and planets continue to roll
on the fingertips of God.
No matter what man does, or doesn't
He's always in control.

THE SANDS OF MY LIFE

Sifting, sifting, shifting, shifting, slipping, slipping,
     gone.
The sands in my glass are going, going fast
and what have I done with the time that I've had?

Liking, liking, loving, loving, losing, losing,
     gone.
The love in my heart is going, going, fast
and who have I now of the people I've loved?

Watching, watching, weeping, weeping, waiting, waiting,
     gone.
The dreams in my mind are going, going fast
and why didn't I try to make them come true?

Crawling, walking, running, walking, creeping.
Dreaming, playing, working, praying, sleeping.
Wanting, getting, using, losing, grieving.
Searching, hoping, asking, trusting, believing

my soul will not die, but will return to God's light of
eternal time, supreme love, and unspeakable happiness.

I will not crawl;
I will fly.

SUMMER OF THE CENTIPEDES

My son arrives with a truckload
of mulch and youthful muscle, begins
removing the old bug-infested bark
from my flower bed. Summer sun
sucks perspiration from his young body.
I slather sun screen on my pre-cancerous

old skin, take cover on the shady
porch white with toxic dust we scattered
to kill the multitudes of creepy centipedes.
"You want something to drink?" I ask.
"I'm ok," he replies. I help him shovel
the old bark onto the trailer for a while,
then suggest we take a break. "Go ahead,

I want to finish this," he smiles. I go
inside to get water, walking carefully. Those
creatures also come inside looking
for a drink, but my floor has become a white,
sandy beach of Borax strewn about
with no ocean in sight, so they curl up
and die in it... or move on. My son is

moving soon, to make his own
home, and I will be left alone. Perhaps I, too
will dehydrate, curl up and bury myself
under the sand. I pick up one live
centipede on a scrap of white paper, open
the door and set him free, sailing off
into the sea-green grass and think,
or maybe someone will arrive in a sailboat
and carry me out to sea, too.

FISHING AT MIDNIGHT

My brain picks the middle of the night
to go fishing. It sets a wiggly worm
on a hook at the end of a line. The words

swim around at this strange, dark time,
as though it were day, with the sun shining,
illuminating each slippery one.

They tease me, jumping on and off the hook,
tangling my line. They call to me, "Catch me!
Catch me!" I must obey. Quickly, before they

get away, I turn on the light, get my pen
and paper, and begin to write.

TREES AT PLAY

Young, red headed oaks
and baby, blonde sweet gums
peek in between
the old, naked knees
of tall dark pines on a morning
so quiet you can hear them laugh,
so cold you can see
their breath.

FIVE WINTER HAIKU

Tires served on a trailer
like chocolate doughnuts, iced
with powdered sugar.

Sturdy trees shudder
as wind skis between them. Snow
falls from their shoulders.

Rain tiptoes in snow,
leaves footprints; icicles
cry from the fascia.

Sugar-coated pine
needles, holly in thorns, iced
rocks, sun exposes.

Sun forces Snowman
into his wet grave; he awaits
resurrection.

BAREFOOT IN THE SNOW

My words walk across the clean, white page
like footprints on a fresh coat of snow.
A cardinal sits on the branch
of a leafless, gray oak like a drop
of blood-red ink. Barefoot truth is cold-cocked,

numbed by the beauty. Snowflakes whisper,
shhh… they're sleeping, as they fall over the buried
tulips and hyacinths. The heat of my steps makes
dark holes in the snow's uniform
cover; the muddy water underneath

seeps out and destroys the once undisturbed
cloak of white purity. But there,
in the thick of the woods, the hungry old buck
still ruts his antlers against a tree.

WHAT DO YOU KNOW OF SPRING?

for Julia

...for what do you know of seasons,
child? of long awaited flowers? You
pluck them without thinking, without knowing
an old woman's joy of looking out
of winter's monochromatic gloom
each morning to find that, yes! the flowers are
in bloom! How could you know
that daffodils and tulips peeking
through green ribbons nod assurance that spring

is here and will stay until the blossoms
fade, dry to brown, and crumble
to dust? But you, in your unbridled lust
for the present, in the wastefulness of youth,
have thoughtlessly, and thoughtfully,
ripped every flower from its stem
and now, with triumphant smile, offer

them—already in the stages of death—
to me as if they were a secret only you
had discovered, but wanted
to share. I turn to hide my tears. Forcing
all of spring into a single vase for a single
day, I feign delight, then you, having done
your good deed, bounce

away. The next morning I hear you call, "Granny!"
I drag my weary bones up, and look out
at the gray yard. Only barren stems and leaves
remain. But then I see your beautiful face, precious
child, smiling at me as if to say... *I
am Spring.*

CIRCLE OF ETERNITY

Time never ends, but lays past and future out of reach
beyond the stars we can see. On Earth we have yet
to discover a way to recover the years of our youth. Still,
some moments feel ever present in our minds. Captured
by a scent, a song, or a taste, we hover a memory
like hummingbirds drunk on the nectar and revisit
again and again to savor that sweet, or sometimes pungent,
flower. Youth, drunk on dreams
set their sights on the future, wish upon a star
for a lover, unsure of who or what
they'll become, while the elderly, unable to see
the future through cataract clouds, dwell in the past
reassured by faith that life is a vapor, that body
is merely a capsule from which the soul will take flight
into its own special light, where absolute peace resides,
where the line of time—what was, is
and ever will be—are joined
to form the circle of eternity.

FISTED RIVER

I cut the ropes and escape
the flood; clouds cover me in wet
kisses as I watch
our homes and crops, cars
and shops as they are surrounded
by the fingers of the river. I look
through the small opening
of its fist. As it closes tighter,
the peephole becomes
smaller… a pinhole, then
nothing. I collapse
in my basket, sailing
through the sea of sky. The clouds
cushion the gathering
ghosts of the dead
buried below. Family. Friends. They whisper
louder and LOUDER. I cover
my ears. Ignoring the rising
river, I adjust
the ropes. Like a salmon at the end
of his journey, I know
the way back.

Made in the USA
Charleston, SC
11 April 2014